Little
Pebble™

Little Critters
Ladybugs

by Lisa J. Amstutz

CAPSTONE PRESS
a capstone imprint

Little Pebble is published by Capstone Press,
1710 Roe Crest Drive, North Mankato, Minnesota 56003
www.mycapstone.com

Library of Congress Cataloging-in-Publication Data
Names: Amstutz, Lisa J., author.
Title: Ladybugs / by Lisa Amstutz.
Description: North Mankato, Minnesota : Capstone Press, [2017] | Series:
  Little pebble. Little critters | Includes bibliographical references and
  index.
Identifiers: LCCN 2016001319| ISBN 9781515719373 (library binding) | ISBN
  9781515719410 (pbk.) | ISBN 9781515719458 (ebook pdf)
Subjects: LCSH: Ladybugs—Juvenile literature.
Classification: LCC QL596.C65 A485 2017 | DDC 595.76/9—dc23
LC record available at http://lccn.loc.gov/2016001319

Editorial Credits
Carrie Braulick Sheely, editor; Juliette Peters, designer;
Wanda Winch, media researcher; Tori Abraham, production specialist

Photo Credits
Ardea.com: Steve Hopkin, 11; Dreamstime: Bereta, 9, Laozhang, 19, Nancykennedy, 15; Shutterstock: Andre Mueller, 17, Bachkova Natalia, 22, Dennis van de Water, 7, Evgeniya Tiplyashina, cover, 5, Henrik Larsson, 13, icarmen13, 1, Igor Sokolov (breeze), back cover, Jan Miko, 21, LianeM, daisy background used throughout book, Maxal Tamor, 20, Oleksandr Kozachenko, 6, picsfive, note design, Valentina Proskurina, back cover (ladybug), 3 (all), 24

Printed in China.
007690

Table of Contents

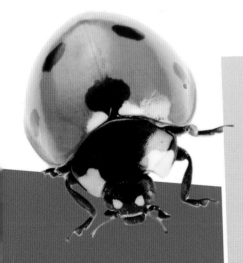

Colors

Look! There is a ladybug!

It is red with black spots.

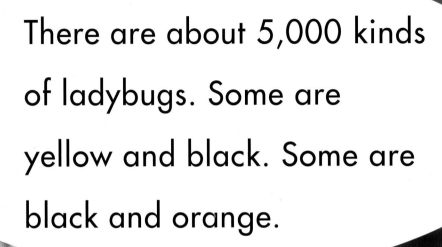

There are about 5,000 kinds of ladybugs. Some are yellow and black. Some are black and orange.

Ladybugs have four wings.

Two are hard and shiny.

Two are soft and clear.

Ladybugs have six legs.

They make stinky goo.

It keeps hungry animals away.

Lunch

Two antennae smell food.
Most ladybugs eat
small bugs.

antennae

Ladybugs are helpers!

They eat pests.

Pests hurt plants.

Growing Up

A ladybug lays tiny eggs.

She hides them under a leaf.

A bumpy larva comes out of each egg. It grows. It sheds its skin.

The larva makes a case.

Inside, it turns into an adult.

It flies away. **Goodbye!**

case

Glossary

adult—fully grown

antenna—a thin part on the head of an insect

larva—an insect at a stage of development between an egg and an adult

pest—an animal that destroys crops humans need or that bothers humans

shed—to let something fall off

Read More

Frisch, Aaron. *Ladybugs.* Mankato, Minn.: Creative Education, 2015.

Gibbons, Gail. *Ladybugs.* New York: Holiday House, 2012.

Mattern, Joanne. *It's a Good Thing There are Ladybugs.* New York: Children's Press, 2015.

Internet Sites

FactHound offers a safe, fun way to find Internet sites related to this book. All of the sites on FactHound have been researched by our staff.

Here's all you do:
Visit *www.facthound.com*
Type in this code: 9781515719373

Check out projects, games and lots more at
www.capstonekids.com

Critical Thinking
Using the Common Core

1. What do ladybugs eat? (Key Ideas and Details)

2. How are ladybugs helpers? (Key Ideas and Details)

Index